Whe People Live

Richard Northcott

Name _____

Age _____

Class _____

OXFORD
UNIVERSITY PRESS

OXFORD
UNIVERSITY PRESS

Great Clarendon Street, Oxford OX2 6DP

Oxford University Press is a department of the University of Oxford.
It furthers the University's objective of excellence in research, scholarship,
and education by publishing worldwide in

Oxford New York

Auckland Bangkok Buenos Aires Cape Town Chennai
Dar es Salaam Delhi Hong Kong Istanbul Karachi Kolkata
Kuala Lumpur Madrid Melbourne Mexico City Mumbai
Nairobi São Paulo Shanghai Taipei Tokyo Toronto

OXFORD and OXFORD ENGLISH are registered trade marks of
Oxford University Press in the UK and in certain other countries

ISBN 0 19 440110 3

Printed in Hong Kong

*The publisher would like to thank the following for kind permission to reproduce
photographs:*

Alamy Images pp 6 (igloo/Bryan & Cherry Alexander Photography), 10 (raised
house/Robert Harding Picture Library), 12 (clay housing/Cosmo Condina), 16 (Venice/Jon
Bower), 24 (tree hut/Anders Ryman); Corbis pp 8 (grass huts/Charles & Josette Lenars),
18 (houseboat/Ric Ergenbright), 30 (winnebago on a desert road/Dave G. Houser); Getty
Images p 14 (cave houses/Ian McKinnell/Taxi); OUP p 2 (chateau); PhotoLibrary.com pp 4
(hut covered in show), 20 (Chinese house courtyard); Punchstock p 22 (room in Japanese
house/PhotoDisc); Rex Features pp 26 (underground house/Mike Daines), 28 (house being
moved/Jennifer Podis)

Illustrations by: Simon Smith (*Illustration p29 by:* Jackie Snider)

With thanks to Sally Spray for her contribution to this series

Reading Dolphins
Notes for teachers & parents

📖 Using the book

1 Begin by looking at the first story page (page 2). Look at the picture and ask questions about it. Then read the story text under the picture with your students. **Use section 1 of the CD for this if possible.**

2 Teach and check the understanding of any new vocabulary. Note that some of the words are in the **Picture Dictionary** at the back of the book.

3 Now look at the activities on the right-hand page. Show the example to the students and instruct them to complete the activities. This may be done individually, in pairs, or as a class.

4 Do the same for the remaining pages of the book.

5 Retell the whole story more quickly, reinforcing the new vocabulary. **Section 2 of the CD can help with this.**

6 **If possible, listen to the expanded story (section 3 of the CD). The students should follow in their books.**

7 When the book is finished, use the **Picture Dictionary** to check that students understand and remember new vocabulary. **Section 4 of the CD can help with this.**

💿 Using the CD

The CD contains four sections.

1 The story told slowly, with pauses. Use this during the first reading. It may also be used for "Listen and repeat" activities at any point.

2 The story told at normal speed. This should be used once the students have read the book for the first time.

3 The expanded story. The story is told in a longer version. This will help the students understand English when it is spoken faster, as they will now know the story and the vocabulary.

4 Vocabulary. Each word in the **Picture Dictionary** is spoken and then used in a simple sentence.

Different people live in different houses.
Let's take a trip around the world and see
how, where, and why people live in
different houses.

Look! This house is called a castle. It is
in France. It is big, old, and beautiful. A
rich person built it, many years ago.

1 Circle ten things that make a house.

(door) picture window freeway stairs
plants living room kitchen floor bathroom
weather roof wall music bedroom

2 Write.

❶ ___door___   ❹ _____

❷ _____   ❺ _____

❸ _____   ❻ _____

3

This house is built high in the mountains in Switzerland. It snows a lot there, in winter. The house is made of wood and stone, and it is very warm inside. The house needs a strong roof because the snow is heavy. The roof is also wide, so it keeps the snow away from the walls.

Answer the questions.

1 Where is this house built?

This house is built in Switzerland

2 How is the weather in winter in this country?

_____

3 What is the house made from?

_____

4 Is the house cold on the inside?

_____

5 Why does it have a strong roof?

_____

6 Do you want to live in a house like this?

_____

7 Why is the roof so wide?

_____

8 Does it snow in your country?

_____

This house is made of big blocks of snow
and it is called an igloo. Igloos look cold
on the outside but they can be really warm
inside.

A hunter can build an igloo for himself
in a few hours, but his dogs have to sleep
outside in the snow.

Write all the nouns and adjectives from page 6 on the igloo.

house

In Africa, where the weather is warmer, some people build houses out of grass and mud. The thick mud walls keep the house nice and cool. The grass on the roof keeps out the heavy rain. There is only one room in each hut. If you want your own room you can build another hut.

Build your own mud hut. Put the sentences in order. Number them 1–8.

☐ Build the walls with the grass and mud.

☐ Get some branches and put them in the ground.

1 Find a place to build your mud hut.

☐ Draw a circle in the sand.

☐ Put grass on the roof.

☐ Make a roof from branches.

☐ Mix grass with mud.

☐ Make a doorway and windows with branches.

In some hot tropical rainforests people build their houses off the ground, on long pieces of wood called stilts. If the house is off the ground, the air can flow under the house and keep it cool. It's also hard for wild animals to come and visit if your house is on stilts.

Circle the correct words.

❶ Stilt houses are built **(in)** / at tropical rainforests.

❷ These houses are built **in** / **on** stilts.

❸ Stilts **is** / **are** long pieces **of** / **a** wood.

❹ Stilt houses **is** / **are** built **on** / **off** the ground.

❺ Air **can** / **cannot** flow **under** / **on** the house.

❻ Wild animals **can** / **cannot** get **in** / **under** the house.

❼ People have to climb **in** / **up** to their stilt house.

❽ There **is** / **are** many stilts under this house.

❾ This house **have** / **has** many big windows.

❿ There **is** / **are** a tree in front of the house.

In very hot dry countries people often build houses out of clay. The houses don't have many windows. The small windows and narrow doors keep the sunshine and the heat out. At night you can sleep up on the flat roof under the moon and stars.

Who lives in which house? Write the correct number next to the name.

Franco [2]　Ella [ ]　Ida [ ]

Peter [ ]　Lina [ ]　David [ ]

Julia [ ]　Marco [ ]　Toni [ ]

Franco's and Ella's houses have white doors.

Ida lives next to Peter.

Marco and Toni have ladders outside their houses.

Peter lives in a house with a black door.

Julia's house has the smallest windows.

Ella lives next to a house with a blue door.

Lina often goes to sleep at David's house because they can sleep on the roof where it is cool.

Toni's house has a blue door and Marco's house has a red door.

Where does Lina live?

Many thousands of years ago, most people lived in caves. They were the first houses. Some people still live in caves, but now they are bigger and more comfortable, and they have doors and windows.
It sometimes takes a long time to build these houses, but they never fall down.

What are the good things and bad things about living in a cave?

Some people like to live near the water.
Venice is in Italy. There are no cars in
Venice, and people get around by boat.
The taxis are boats, and even the buses
are boats.

Would you like to go to school by boat?

Circle the correct words.

1 (This) / These is Maria.

2 She live / **lives** in Venice.

3 **His** / Her house is on the water.

4 There **is** / are no cars in Venice.

5 People **go** / goes to work by boat.

6 Maria go / **goes** to school by water bus.

7 Her father have / **has** a boat, too.

8 He take / **takes** visitors around Venice in his boat.

9 Maria likes to ride / **rides** in her father's boat.

10 Living near the water **is** / are a lot of fun.

17

Some people live in a house and some people work on a boat. These lucky people in India live on a houseboat. Houseboats are usually made of wood and they are often very beautiful. People cook, wash, eat, and sleep on their boats.

Check ☑ true or false.

		True	False
❶	Some people live in houseboats.	☑	☐
❷	Houseboats can move around.	☐	☐
❸	A houseboat has a kitchen.	☐	☐
❹	Only people in India live in houseboats.	☐	☐
❺	People only live in houseboats in summer.	☐	☐
❻	Houseboats are usually made of wood.	☐	☐
❼	The houseboat in the picture has some stairs.	☐	☐
❽	People only sleep on houseboats.	☐	☐
❾	A houseboat is smaller than a house.	☐	☐
❿	You live on a houseboat.	☐	☐

Some houses have a special shape. This Chinese house has three sides, built around a courtyard. In the past, Chinese people had big families. The grandparents lived in one part of the house, and the parents and children lived in other parts. On special days they all got together in the courtyard.

Look at the family tree. Men are shown by 男 and women by 女. Complete the sentences.

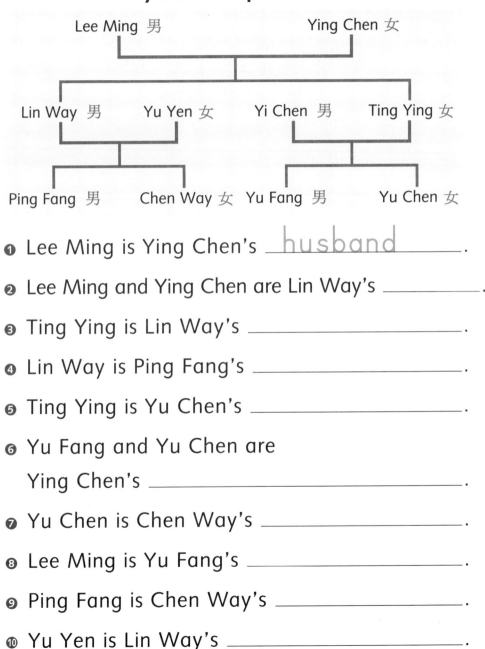

Lee Ming 男   Ying Chen 女

Lin Way 男   Yu Yen 女   Yi Chen 男   Ting Ying 女

Ping Fang 男   Chen Way 女   Yu Fang 男   Yu Chen 女

❶ Lee Ming is Ying Chen's __husband__.

❷ Lee Ming and Ying Chen are Lin Way's _____.

❸ Ting Ying is Lin Way's _____.

❹ Lin Way is Ping Fang's _____.

❺ Ting Ying is Yu Chen's _____.

❻ Yu Fang and Yu Chen are
   Ying Chen's _____.

❼ Yu Chen is Chen Way's _____.

❽ Lee Ming is Yu Fang's _____.

❾ Ping Fang is Chen Way's _____.

❿ Yu Yen is Lin Way's _____.

21

In some parts of the world people have to be careful how they build their houses. In Japan there are many earthquakes. In the past Japanese people built their houses out of wood and paper, because they are light. In an earthquake, a house like this is safer than a house made of bricks or stone.

Did you know?

Japanese homes are not very big, so Japanese people don't often have guests stay in their homes.

Japanese take off their shoes in the house. There is a special place to take off your shoes called a *genkan*.

Some rooms have mats made from rice-straw on the floor, called *tatami*.

It is polite to tell everybody when you arrive home or before you leave home.

Japanese people wash with soap and water first, then they get into the bath.

Japanese people sleep on beds called *futon*. These are laid out on the *tatami* floor. When people wake up they pack the *futon* away in a cupboard, to make more space in the room.

Japanese people have special slippers for use in the toilet. If you don't see a pair of slippers outside the toilet, then you know someone is inside.

Some houses can be a lot of fun. Can you imagine climbing a tree to get into your house? These people live in a tree house, because it's cooler, safer, and really high up. This tree house is in Papua New Guinea. The view from up there is really wonderful.

What can you see from a tree house? Look at the picture. Use these words.

sky mountains river cloud bear
nest eagle butterfly trunk branch
leaves ground

sky

If you don't want to live in a tree, you can always live underground. This strange house in England is built to save energy. The thick walls are covered in grass and the windows are in the roof. It's warm in the winter and cool in the summer. What a great place to live!

Which mail goes to which house? Connect.

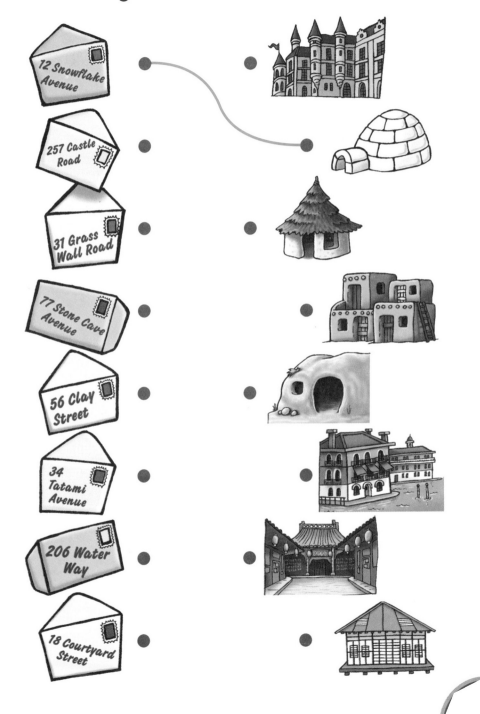

If you really like your house, but you have to move, why not take your house with you? This is how you do it. You need a truck and a very big trailer. You put your house on the trailer and take it to your new address. You must drive slowly and watch out for low bridges!

Follow the directions for moving house.
Where do you move to? Find and draw.

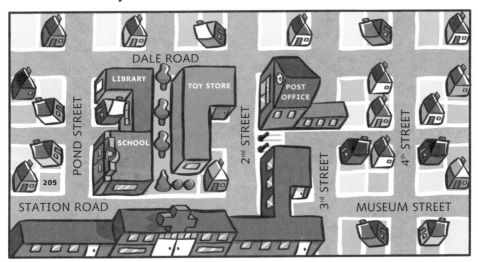

❶ Your old house is at 205 Pond Street. You want to move your house to a new address on a truck.

❷ You drive up to Dale Road. Turn right into Dale Road. Go straight for four blocks.

❸ Turn right into 4th street. Go straight down 4th street for two blocks.

❹ Turn right into Museum Street and go straight for one block.

❺ Turn right into 3rd Street. Your new address is on the right side of the road.

❻ Draw your house at your new address.

If you like to travel around and see different places, this is the best home for you. It has everything from a bathroom to a kitchen, and a bedroom to a living room – it even has wheels.

So you can drive across the country without ever leaving your home!

Complete.

People __live__ in different _____

around the world.

The biggest house we saw was the

_____ in _____.

In cold places people built igloos made of

_____.

In Africa some people make houses with

_____.

In _____ some people live on the water

in _____.

Some people build houses in _____ and

others live under _____.

I like the _____ most, because

_____

_____

_____.

Picture Dictionary

bear   butterfly

boat   castle

branch   cave

brick   courtyard

bridge   eagle

grass

snow

igloo

stairs

ladder

trailer

mountain

truck

roof

trunk

Dolphin Readers

Dolphin Readers are available at five levels, from Starter to 4.

The Dolphins series covers four major themes:

Grammar, Living Together, The World Around Us, Science and Nature.

For each theme, there are two titles at every level.

Activity Books are available for all Dolphins.

All Dolphins are available on audio CD.
(2 TITLES ON EACH CD ⊙ SEE TABLE BELOW)

Teacher's Notes are available at **www.oup.com/elt/dolphins**

	Grammar	Living Together	The World Around Us	Science and Nature
Starter	• Silly Squirrel • Monkeying Around ⊙	• My Family • A Day with Baby ⊙	• Doctor, Doctor • Moving House ⊙	• A Game of Shapes • Baby Animals ⊙
Level 1	• Meet Molly • Where Is It? ⊙	• Little Helpers • Jack the Hero ⊙	• On Safari • Lost Kitten ⊙	• Number Magic • How's the Weather? ⊙
Level 2	• Double Trouble • Super Sam ⊙	• Candy for Breakfast • Lost! ⊙	• A Visit to the City • Matt's Mistake ⊙	• Numbers, Numbers Everywhere • Circles and Squares ⊙
Level 3	• Students in Space • What Did You Do Yesterday? ⊙	• New Girl in School • Uncle Jerry's Great Idea ⊙	• Just Like Mine • Wonderful Wild Animals ⊙	• Things That Fly • Let's Go to the Rainforest ⊙
Level 4	• The Tough Task • Yesterday, Today and Tomorrow ⊙	• We Won the Cup • Up and Down ⊙	• Where People Live • City Girl, Country Boy ⊙	• In the Ocean • Go, Gorillas, Go ⊙

Let's G[o to]
the Rainforest

Fiona Kenshole

Name _____

Age _____

Class _____

OXFORD
UNIVERSITY PRESS

OXFORD
UNIVERSITY PRESS

Great Clarendon Street, Oxford OX2 6DP

Oxford University Press is a department of the University of Oxford.
It furthers the University's objective of excellence in research, scholarship,
and education by publishing worldwide in

Oxford New York

Auckland Bangkok Buenos Aires Cape Town Chennai
Dar es Salaam Delhi Hong Kong Istanbul Karachi Kolkata
Kuala Lumpur Madrid Melbourne Mexico City Mumbai
Nairobi São Paulo Shanghai Taipei Tokyo Toronto

OXFORD and OXFORD ENGLISH are registered trade marks of
Oxford University Press in the UK and in certain other countries

© Oxford University Press 2005

ISBN 0 19 440106 5

Printed in Hong Kong

*The publisher would like to thank the following for kind permission
to reproduce photographs:*

Corbis pp 6 (sun breaking through treetops/Darrell Gulin), 22 (deforestation/Wayne
Lawler); Frank Lane Picture Agency pp 16 (butterfly/Michael & Patricia fogden/Minden
Pictures), 16 (red bug/Mark Moffett/Minden Pictures); Getty Images p 4 (boat on rainforest
river/Michael Melford/Image Bank), Nature Picture Library p 14 (ants on a
leaf/Premaphotos); PhotoLibrary.com pp 2 (rainforest), 10 (ring-tailed lemur), 12 (green
tree frog), 16 (metallic wood-boring beatle), 16 (morpho butterfly), 18 (jaguar), 20 (bat at
night), 8 (three parrots on branch/Johner).

Illustrations by: Jackie Snider

With thanks to Sally Spray for her contribution to this series

📖 Using the book

1 Begin by looking at the first story page (page 2). Look at the picture and ask questions about it. Then read the story text under the picture with your students. Use section 1 of the CD for this if possible.

2 Teach and check the understanding of any new vocabulary. Note that some of the words are in the **Picture Dictionary** at the back of the book.

3 Now look at the activities on the right-hand page. Show the example to the students and instruct them to complete the activities. This may be done individually, in pairs, or as a class.

4 Do the same for the remaining pages of the book.

5 Retell the whole story more quickly, reinforcing the new vocabulary. Section 2 of the CD can help with this.

6 If possible, listen to the expanded story (section 3 of the CD). The students should follow in their books.

7 When the book is finished, use the **Picture Dictionary** to check that students understand and remember new vocabulary. Section 4 of the CD can help with this.

💿 Using the CD

The CD contains four sections.

1 The story told slowly, with pauses. Use this during the first reading. It may also be used for "Listen and repeat" activities at any point.

2 The story told at normal speed. This should be used once the students have read the book for the first time.

3 The expanded story. The story is told in a longer version. This will help the students understand English when it is spoken faster, as they will now know the story and the vocabulary.

4 Vocabulary. Each word in the **Picture Dictionary** is spoken and then used in a simple sentence.

This is a rainforest.
The weather here is hot all year.
It is always wet.
It rains every day.
It feels hot and sticky.

1 Circle yes or no .

❶ Rainforests are wet.   (yes)   no

❷ There are trees in a rainforest.   yes   no

❸ It never rains in the rainforest.   yes   no

❹ There are animals in the rainforest.   yes   no

❺ It's always cold in the rainforest.   yes   no

❻ It's easy to travel in the rainforest.   yes   no

❼ There are rivers in the rainforest.   yes   no

❽ Rainforests are important to us.   yes   no

2 Complete.

A rainforest is _____ , _____ ,

and _____ .

Let's go to the rainforest.
First you fly in an airplane.
Then you ride in a truck.
Then you go in a boat.
Finally you walk.

1 **How to grow a tree. Put the sentences in order. Number them 1 to 6.**

☐ Cover the seed with soil.

☐ Dig a hole.

1 Buy a seed.

☐ Find a good place in the garden.

☐ Put the seed in the hole.

☐ Water the soil.

2 **How to grow a tree. Complete.**

First, you buy a seed.

Then _____

Then _____

Then _____

Finally _____

Trees in the rainforest grow very tall.
The tops of the trees can reach
the clouds.
The trees live a long time.
They can live a thousand years.

Number.

7	bark		snake		plant
	root		trunk		bird
	flower		branch		butterfly
	fruit		leaf		soil

Many birds and animals live in
the rainforest.
Sometimes you cannot see them
because it is dark under the trees.
But you can often hear them.

Complete the puzzle.

1 | b | i | r | d
2
3
4
5
6
7
8
9
10

All these animals live in the

r_____.

9

What are these strange-looking animals?

They are a family of lemurs. Lemurs come out at night and they use their big eyes to look for fruit.

How many lemurs can you see?

Connect.

 Elephants use big ears •

 Alligators use strong tails •

 Eagles use big wings •

 Piranhas use sharp teeth •

 Monkeys use long tails •

 Anacondas use their body •

 Lemurs use big eyes •

 Tigers use black stripes •

• to swim quickly.

• to fly through the air.

• to them keep cool.

• to swing in the trees.

• to eat their food.

• to find fruit.

• to hide in the grass.

• to kill their prey.

Tree frogs are very small.
This tree frog lives in a flower.
Tree frogs are bright and colorful.
This frog has big eyes and a
big mouth.

1 Write about this elephant.

Elephants _____

very _____ .

This _____ lives

_____ _____

rainforest. _____ _____ gray.

This elephant _____ a long

_____ and _____ ears.

2 Write about this parrot.

Parrots _____ quite

_____ .

This _____ _____

in _____ _____ .

Parrots are bright _____ _____ .

This _____ has a _____

_____ and _____ wings.

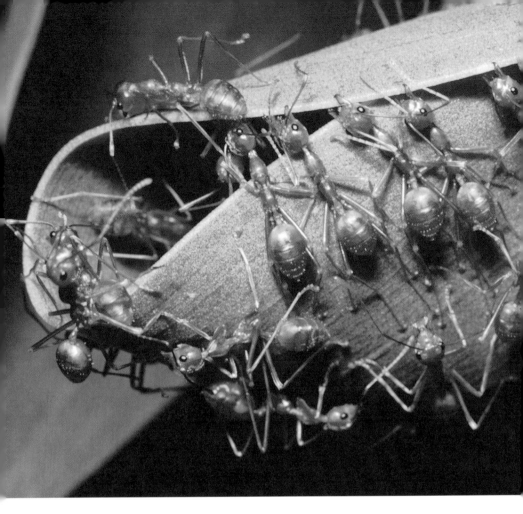

The rainforest is home to millions of ants. They are always very busy. Although they are small, they are very strong when they work together as a group.

Connect the animal with the description.

an anaconda •

an ant •

a bat •

a jaguar •

a frog •

a lemur •

a jaguar •

a monkey •

a piranha •

• can live in water and on land

• is a very big snake

• is the king of the rainforest

• sleeps upside down

• can run very fast

• looks for food at night

• is very good at climbing

• is a fish with sharp teeth

• is very small, but very strong

Insects, insects, they are everywhere. There are more insects in the rainforest than any other animal. They come in all shapes, colors, and sizes. Each insect is different, but they all have six legs.

1 Circle the insect words.

 grasshopper

 cockroach

 dragonfly

 fly

 moth

```
G R A S S H O P P E R
I N S E F L Y C D T S
B E E T L E A R R E S
M A C O C K R O A C H
L L B U T V E R G R O
Y M O S Q U I T O I R
I O M P O R T A N C N
N T T A B N I M F K E
A H L S E Z Z Z L E T
B U T T E R F L Y T Z
```

 mosquito

 cricket

 beetle

bee

 hornet

 butterfly

2 Write the hidden sentence from the uncircled letters.

I _ _ _ _ _ _ _ _ _ _ _ _ _

_ _ _ _ _ _ _ _ _ _ _ _ _ .

17

This big cat is a jaguar. It's the king of the rainforest. It hunts through the trees, using its ears, eyes, and nose to find an animal to eat. It's strong and fast – and very dangerous.

1 Connect the animals to their verbs.

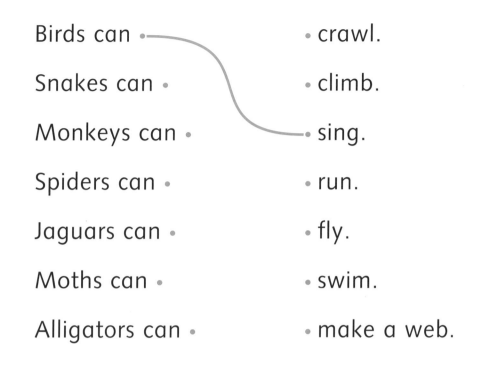

Birds can •   • crawl.

Snakes can •   • climb.

Monkeys can •   • sing.

Spiders can •   • run.

Jaguars can •   • fly.

Moths can •   • swim.

Alligators can •   • make a web.

2 Answer the questions.

❶ Which animals can run?

Jaguars can run.

❷ Which animals can sing?

_____

❸ Which animals can make a web?

_____

It's night-time in the rainforest.
The moon is shining.
What's that? It's a bat!
Bats sleep in the day and fly around
at night.

Answer the questions.

❶ When do bats sleep?

Bats sleep in the day.

❷ Where does the tree frog live?

_____

❸ How long do some trees live?

_____

❹ How's the weather in a rainforest?

_____

❺ What do lemurs eat?

_____

❻ Why can't you see some animals?

_____

The rainforest is very important to all of us. It cleans the air, and is home to many animals and plants. If we protect the rainforest, we can help save the world.

How can we protect the rainforest?
Check ✔ six sentences.

- ☐ Drink a lot of water.
- ☐ Do your homework.
- ✔ Don't waste paper.
- ☐ Eat your vegetables.
- ☐ Stop cutting down trees.
- ☐ Don't watch too much TV.
- ☐ Teach people about the rainforest.
- ☐ Plant more trees.
- ☐ Don't use wood to build houses.
- ☐ Ride a bicycle and don't drive a car.

Picture Dictionary

alligator

butterfly

ant

frog

bark

jaguar

bat

leaf

branch

monkey

parrot

spider

root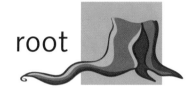

tiger

seed

truck

snake

Dolphin Readers

Dolphin Readers are available at five levels, from Starter to 4.

The Dolphins series covers four major themes:

Grammar, Living Together, The World Around Us, Science and Nature.

For each theme, there are two titles at every level.

Activity Books are available for all Dolphins.

All Dolphins are available on audio CD.
(2 TITLES ON EACH CD SEE TABLE BELOW)

Teacher's Notes are available at **www.oup.com/elt/dolphins**

	Grammar	Living Together	The World Around Us	Science and Nature
Starter	• Silly Squirrel • Monkeying Around	• My Family • A Day with Baby	• Doctor, Doctor • Moving House	• A Game of Shapes • Baby Animals
Level 1	• Meet Molly • Where Is It?	• Little Helpers • Jack the Hero	• On Safari • Lost Kitten	• Number Magic • How's the Weather?
Level 2	• Double Trouble • Super Sam	• Candy for Breakfast • Lost!	• A Visit to the City • Matt's Mistake	• Numbers, Numbers Everywhere • Circles and Squares
Level 3	• Students in Space • What Did You Do Yesterday?	• New Girl in School • Uncle Jerry's Great Idea	• Just Like Mine • Wonderful Wild Animals	• Things That Fly • Let's Go to the Rainforest
Level 4	• The Tough Task • Yesterday, Today and Tomorrow	• We Won the Cup • Up and Down	• Where People Live • City Girl, Country Boy	• In the Ocean • Go, Gorillas, Go